PRACTICAL TIPS FOR PARENTING

Equipping Families for Positive Living

Inez V. Harrison

authorHOUSE®

AuthorHouse™ LLC
1663 Liberty Drive
Bloomington, IN 47403
www.authorhouse.com
Phone: 1-800-839-8640

Published by AuthorHouse 03/06/2014

ISBN: 978-1-4918-5396-2 (sc)
ISBN: 978-1-4918-5394-8 (e)

Library of Congress Control Number: 2014901124

CONTENTS

Chapter 5

Chapter 6

Chapter 7

Chapter 8

Chapter 9

Chapter 10

Chapter 11

Chapter 12

Chapter 13

Chapter 14

Chapter 15

Chapter 16

I dedicate this book to my sister, Florence Harrison, whom I love. I so appreciate her inspiration and encouragement. Our combined years of experience working with youth and families helped to produce a book that we believe is a message and a teaching that has greatly influenced not only our lives but the lives of the families we have touched and taught and who have discovered what it means to be equipped for positive living. What a treasure to have a sister like her.

I also dedicate this book to my sister, Victoria Archer, who has been instrumental in implementing our Nurturing Generation to Generation program.

In addition, I dedicate this book to my fourteen brothers and sisters whom I love. They have influenced my life in more ways than I can say.

Finally, I dedicate this book to my deceased parents. Were it not for their being such truly godly parents and leading us into positive living, we would not be the family we are today. Thank you, Mom and Dad, for giving us the life intended for families everywhere.

A house is built through wisdom and is established by understanding. Your children are filled with all precious and pleasant riches through the knowledge you give and the examples you set.

INTRODUCTION

Families need to be educated on how to deal with one another. You can actually learn to alter your and your children's feelings and attitudes. New nurturing behaviors can replace hurtful ones that could cost your children emotionally. I am sure you would rather build happy, healthy interactions in your family than live with problems no one ever taught you to solve.

I was moved after a visit to a county juvenile delinquency court where I heard young people and parents crying out for help in their communication process. These children felt they were not being heard and parents were at their wits end. For many of the parents, their own life experience had not set the best of examples and no one had offered them Parenting 101. As a result, hit and miss, and trial and error had led them and their young teens to the courthouse. For the teens, inability to follow appropriate guidelines, lack of consistent discipline, the inability to take responsibility for their appropriate and inappropriate behavior, and disrespect were leading them down a wrong path. It was certain that parents needed practical tips, tools, and guidelines at their disposal.

Do you want a home where there is warmth, trust, care, and respect? Do you want a home that creates an environment for self-development for each of your children? Do you want assistance with elevating love, acceptance, and self-esteem in your home? Do you want help with developing and teaching positive communication in your home? Are you looking for effective strategies for resolving conflicts, encouraging cooperative responsible behavior, and managing challenging behavior in your children? Are you looking for insight into how feelings influence your children's behavior?

By the time you finish this book, you will have keys to establish and practice positive experiences within your home. Keys for the ever-increasing flow of love in your home, keys for enhancing good self-esteem in your children, keys for expressing feelings responsibly, keys for fostering conversation with your family, keys for listening well, keys for smoothing out the bumps in family life, and keys for family cooperation—responsibility, respect, rules, and family meetings.

Children are the diamonds that put the sparkle in our eyes and in the eyes of their grandparents. The love that flows between parents and their children and positive, effective communication in families keeps that sparkle aglow.

You are the primary influence on how your children feel about themselves. How they build their lives begins with you. Your children must know they are valued. They must know how you see them. Who they are is a mirror of you. We must provide a positive reflection. Your children were born with purpose. They are filled with all precious and pleasant riches through the knowledge you give and examples you set.

Parents are to direct their children and their households rightly and justly. The sphere of our influence begins with what we are taught and continues throughout our lifetime. It is never ending.

God chooses each parent with great care and entrusts your children to your specific care. Scripture says, "I have chosen him (Abraham), so that he will direct his children and his household after him to keep the way of the Lord by doing what is right and just" (Genesis 18:19). The sphere of our influence begins with what we teach them about God and continues throughout their lifetime. It is never ending.

Your ultimate inescapable responsibility is to shape your children's attitudes, actions, relationships, and discipline. When we are consistent in delivering positive instruction and wisdom to our children, we practice the best kind of parenting. When we place unreasonable demands and abuse our authority, our parenting is ineffective. When we make anything more important than our children are, we take another step away from love. As our children mature, we want them to develop a habit of doing right and making their own decisions and accepting responsibility for their choices, even the poor ones. If our children learn from their mistakes and accept correction, they are on the right course.

Impress your standards and values on your children. Talk about these values when you sit with your children at home, when you ride around with them, when you lie down, and when you get up. Write them down and post them for everyone to see. In Deuteronomy 6:9, he told Israel to write down his commands. Get them inside of you and then get them inside your children. Talk about them wherever you are, sitting at home or walking in the street; talk about them from the time you get up in the morning to the time you fall into bed at night. Tie them on your hands and foreheads as a reminder; inscribe them on the doorposts of your homes and on your city gates.

Home is the place where love begins, where we find agreement and purpose, and where we build character. Our children learn about their world through watching and imitating us. What we give them passes from generation to generation.

CHAPTER 1

LOVE! OUR CHILDREN'S DESTINY-THE MUSIC THAT BRINGS HARMONY

In family life, love is the oil that eases friction, the cement that binds closer together, and the music that brings harmony.—Eva Burrows[1]

Our demonstrated love is our children's destiny. We give the legacy to them and to their children. They are extensions of our parents, and us, and ultimately of God himself. They are not perfect, neither are we, but we must love them. I cannot tell you that there were not times when I felt it might be better if somehow I could return the young treasures God had given me, but I never failed to remember that he had entrusted me to them. Therefore, I worked diligently on building character in them, on praising and encouraging them, on discerning and listening to their feelings, on solving problems, and on creating an environment of trust, care, and respect. I had no doubt that my expressions and my example of true love would transcend into them and into my future generations in a positive way. Nurturing children is about the way we love them. Nurturing is one of the most important things we can do.

Teach your children about the love of God, and share with them what he thinks of them. Have them confess: "I am God's workmanship (handiwork) created (born anew) in Christ to do His work that He planned beforehand that I should do" (Ephesians 2:10).

Remind them they are an expression of the life of Christ because he is their life.

As a little girl, I experienced love continually in our home. My father gave each of us an endearing name that was personal. He called me his dark-eyed beauty. That may not seem much to you, but to me, as a middle child who had some self-image issues, it was big. So often I saw the beauty in everyone else in the family but could not see it in myself. Yet, continually, I would hear the endearing words of my father in my head. He saw my inner beauty, and after a time I began to embrace who he said I was. What he saw, Father God saw. It resulted in my continually reminding my sons of what I see inside of them and ultimately how God sees them.

The love and care we give to our children determines how our children will grow up and how they will eventually parent. Most research indicates that parenting is learned in childhood and is repeated when children become parents.[2] The experiences children have while growing up significantly affect attitudes, skills, and the parenting practices they will use.[3] I, too, believe that the way children are raised directly influences the way they will raise their children.

Tips for Increasing the Flow of Love in Your Home

Declare a love week. Have your family members write down (or draw) what makes them feel loved. Maybe your first grader feels loved when you read to him. Maybe your teenage daughter feels loved when you go shopping with her. Post the ideas in the house where everyone will see them. Then, every day for the next week, encourage family members to do something for another family member that helps them feel loved.

Write love notes. Write short notes of love and encouragement and put them in your children's lunchboxes or backpacks. Examples may include, "Thanks for helping your brother clean up his room." "That was a good idea you had for our family vacation." "You're special to me." "Will you come with me to the store when you get home from school?" "I enjoy having you with me."

Make sure each person feels loved. Children like to receive love in a different way, so send that love in the way that matters to them. It is good to pay attention to how your child shows love and to what your child wants to do more of with you. You can also ask your children what you do that helps them feel loved. This is the only way you can be assured that your actions won't be perceived as unloving. I read a story about a mother who came home from a long day at work, met her little boy at the front door, pinched his cheek, told him "I love you!" and walked to her room. He followed her and replied, "Mommy, I don't want you to love me, I want you to play a game with me!"

A loving touch. Don't hesitate to give your child a loving hug, a comforting hand squeeze, or a congratulatory pat on the back. It can make an important difference.

Establishing and Modeling Standards

Children have more need of models than of critics.—Carolyn Coats[4]

A wise parent establishes what will or will not be in the house. They set standards, believe in the value of each family member, and never give up on any family member. Every family member must learn to share and accept one another's good and bad qualities. Godly standards, his commands, are the most appropriate standards that we must teach our children.

When I taught high school, a number of students came to or stayed in my classroom after school. They just wanted to chat. They would tell me how much they appreciated the time I took to help them to set limits in their lives. These guidelines helped to shape their decisions. Those who had freedom to do as they pleased, expressed they felt their parents did not really care about them. Though they often rebelled, most expressed they felt much more cared about when their parents set down rules for them. Children need and respond to age-appropriate standards and boundaries. It is a demonstration of care and interest and authority.

When we instruct our children, we are not simply presenting a list of rules to follow. We let our actions speak. As a parent, you are the teaching model. Teach your children to serve one another. Sometimes this means sacrificing their own wants. The family who celebrates one another's joys—birthdays, births and deaths, graduations, weddings, holidays, new jobs, family reunions, surprise visits—are families who rarely fall apart. Encourage them to listen and respond appropriately to one another.

Model forgiveness. Let your children observe forgiveness in action. When someone pushes you or hits you by accident, let your children hear you sincerely say to the person, "It's okay, no problem, don't worry about it." Very easily and lovingly, accept apologies. Let your children see you being helpful to people who have offended you. They become accustomed to your being the peacemaker. They observe you in traffic. Even if your children don't always practice what you do, we know they have the right model implanted in their hearts.

Treat children according to their needs. Children need their parents to notice and appreciate their special qualities. Each child is different and has different needs. My youngest son loved to read books, especially the *World Almanac*. He loved to keep abreast with those who faced and overcame great challenges, so we shared important times of discovery. My oldest son, on the other hand, was very artistic and loved to draw, so we shopped together for the right pencils and sketchpads for his drawings. He loved to have me stand with him in the window and make comments on the scenes of nature that he so loved to draw. One day, when I phoned my twelve-year-old grandson, he told me he was so excited about the Nike and McDonald stocks. I jumped on it and told my son to encourage and nurture that interest in his son. Help him to learn about the economy, the bull and bear markets, and anything else of interest in that area. Who knows what is inside of him. My participation in sharing their interests demonstrated to them that I valued their special qualities.

Loving Yourself

As a parent, you need to fulfill your parenting role and as an individual with interests outside the family. Go places on your own and do some things just for yourself. Find a balance between meeting your children's needs and making time for yourselves.

The kids were off to school, and I took my "me time." It was so much fun gathering new ideas and creating new projects. Then I was off to my fitness class. As quickly as I could, I took a quick shower, jumped in my car, and raced toward the school parking lot. There I sat waiting to see my sons come running out of the building. My workout and macramé classes had refreshed me, renewed my energy, and seemed to make me more enthusiastically available to my children.

What a positive difference in the way I felt. I was ready to listen to all of their stories and work with their never-ending energy.

It is also important for you to find appropriate outlets for your feelings of stress and responsibilities. Don't let stress overtake you. Call a trusted friend and express how you're feeling. Take the children to someone or ask him or her to come over and stay with the kids for a while. It is rejuvenating to take short breaks from your children.

Chapter 2

Challenging Unhealthy Beliefs and Strengthening Healthy Beliefs

It's not the events of our lives that shape us, but
our beliefs as to what those events mean.
—Tony Robbins[1]

Do you have the right belief system about your parenting? Check your beliefs and begin to work on those that need changing. Unhealthy and healthy beliefs teach principles to your children. Healthy beliefs are more flexible about preferences, whereas unhealthy beliefs are usually rigid and involve demands or rules.

Challenging Unhealthy Beliefs

Ask yourself whether this belief is false or inconsistent with reality. Is it rigid, extreme, or illogical? You could also attempt to determine where the belief came from. Try thinking about whether you would want a close friend to hold such a belief. Unhealthy beliefs about parenting can discourage you and create problems in your parenting.

Strengthening Healthy Beliefs

To strengthen your healthy beliefs, move them from your head to your heart. Consider whether the belief is true and consistent with reality. Is it <u>flexible</u> and balanced? Does it make sense? How does it affect me emotionally? Healthy beliefs teach us how we ought to think of ourselves and how we ought to think about our parenting.

Tips for Reviewing Your Belief System

Unhealthy Belief Statements

- My children's love and approval is the most important thing in life.
- I should never make mistakes with my children.
- Children must always be well behaved.
- I have failed as a parent if my children do not behave.
- I am completely responsible for my children's problems.
- My children should not make mistakes.
- I get cooperation if I continue to criticize, nag, and lecture.
- My children cause me to be angry, frustrated, and anxious.
- It is easier to avoid rather than face life's difficulties and responsibilities.
- My happiness is dependent on my being in control of things.
- Crisis automatically sets in when things don't go the way I planned.

Healthy Belief Statements

- The most important thing in life for my children is acceptance of who they are. Truly get to know them. Know their likes and dislikes, perceive, and discern their thoughts. Be thoroughly familiar with their ways.
- I must raise my children appropriately and trust that the results will be good.
- The training I give will forever be with my child.
- I model. This will guide my children.

- Be confident that my efforts will be richly rewarded.
- I train, but it takes time for my children to acquire a disciplined and prudent life.
- Children acquire a disciplined and prudent life—doing what is right, just, and fair.
- There will be times when what I have taught my children seems somehow stolen, dead, even destroyed, but in the end, the training I give will result in a full and complete life.
- Uncontrolled words only cause arguments.
- Foolish and stupid arguments produce quarrels. Instead of the quarrels, I must be kind to everyone, able to teach by example, and I must not be resentful.
- I must not let any unwholesome talk come out of my mouth. I must be helpful and build up my children according to their needs that may bring true benefit.
- I am responsible for my own emotions.
- I must rule my own heart. When I make a real effort to know and understand, I will be calm.
- I will teach and admonish my children with wisdom.
- Sometimes my plans may fail, but I must keep going.

CHAPTER 3

WHAT IS YOUR PARENTING STYLE?

Life affords no greater responsibility, no greater
privilege, than the raising of the next generation
—C. Everett Koop[1]

The home is where we find agreement and purpose. Here is where you build and teach character. Here is where love begins. Children need guidance; they learn about their world through watching and imitating you. How you were parented may not have been the best way to parent. Your parenting style is usually a result of your own upbringing and your role models. Your style affects the way you interact with your children. Knowing your style, its strengths, weaknesses, and its possible affects on your children and making adjustments where necessary, will help your children become responsible loving adults. There are three different parenting styles— authoritarian, permissive, and self-governing-authoritative.[2]

Authoritarian parents control all their children's behavior—right or wrong. If you are an authoritarian, you will likely equate discipline with strictness or sometimes harshness. You expect them to follow your directions without question or need for explanation. Authoritarian parents expect their children to accept, without question, their goals, values, and beliefs. Authoritarians take charge, initiate, enjoy challenges, and expect results. On the other hand, authoritarians feel a need to control their environment and often have poor social skills. They can be strict, inflexible, and even domineering. Your children are likely to remain passive until they leave home. Children of authoritarians often are angry and aggressive. They can be dependent on external controls. Their low self-esteem can lead to depression. On the other hand, children of authoritarian parents generally perform moderately well in school and usually don't exhibit problem behavior.

Permissive parents have love as their motivating factor. Love is the most important thing in their relationship with their children. They spend a lot of time with the <u>child</u> communicating, negotiating, reasoning, and making their child feel special. Permissive parents generally do not deny their children's requests. They set few or no limits for their children, which can result in unacceptable behavior. Their children often manipulate permissive parents. Permissive parents have to watch that they do not worry about their children rejecting them. Permissive parents are compassionate, encouraging, supportive, and accepting. They must be careful of being lax and too lenient. Permissive parenting promotes feelings of insecurity in children. Insecure children can become discouraged. Children raised by permissive parents can perform poorly at school, misbehave frequently, and are sometimes rebellious and unable to conform to rules. They can also be demanding. On the other hand, children of permissive parents are likely to have better social skills and higher self-esteem.

Self-governing parents are generally responsive yet firm. These parents integrate a balance between encouraging individuality and independence and setting guidelines for their children's behavior depending on their children's attributes, abilities, and development level. A self-governing-authoritative parent sets guidelines with their children so they have a clear understanding of what the rules of the home include. When making demands, they accompany those demands with explanations to help the child understand. They use reason and discussion and will even negotiate when they deem it necessary. They praise worthy behavior and achievement. Because these children generally want to live in harmony, they comply or at least learn how to constructively dissent in an effort to change their parents' minds. These children develop mutual respect, responsibility, self-discipline, and problem-solving skills. Self-governing parenting solidly reinforces a value system that includes honesty, integrity, caring, compassion, kindness, and empathy. Children of self-governing parents are likely well behaved, self-reliant, and socially successful.

Tip for Parenting Styles

- Remember, no parenting style is right or wrong. There are times you will flow from one to another depending on the situation. It is important to have balance.

Chapter 4

Be a Nurturing Parent

Your family and your love must be cultivated like a garden.
Time, effort, and imagination must be summoned constantly to
keep any relationship flourishing and growing.—Jim Rohn[1]

Raising your children is the most important job you will ever have. It is likely your children will do exceptionally well when both parents are actively involved in their upbringing. Each parent brings a unique aspect to the children.

Loving Father

Fathering is not something perfect men do, but something that perfects the man.—Frank Pittman, *Enough.*[2]

Always be truthful and sincere. Direct your children and your household in what is right and just. Deal with your children by encouraging, comforting, and urging them to live full and wonderful lives. Do not provoke your children to become angry.

Be like Paul in scripture, "For you know that we dealt with each of you as a father deals with his own children, encouraging, comforting, and urging you to live lives worthy of God, who calls you into his kingdom, and glory" (1 Thessalonians 2:11-12). Also in 1 Thessalonians 2:7, "We were gentle among you, like a nursing mother caring for her little children."

Stand solid as a rock in the home. Be strong in the good times and in the bad. Be the unshakable one; realize that your consistency brings strength to the family. When you make a decision, stick by it. If you make mistakes, be willing to admit it. Honesty and humility are not signs of weakness, rather of strength. Your children will imitate you.

Your children and grandchildren put the finishing touches on you. They bring you great joy and fill your heart with love. Your children are taught integrity when you walk in integrity. This sets a path for your children's success.

Stand as head of the home and take the lead in your family. You are responsible for the primary provision of your household: sheltering, feeding, clothing, and educating your family. Love is the reason for discipline. Forgive, be compassionate, and show mercy. Compassion and forgiveness are important keys. Often you have to show mercy even when you do not feel like you want to. You must responsibly watch over the family's growth and development. You are responsible to gather your family for family meetings. Watch the attitude and character development of each person in your home. Provide wholesome recreation, good books, monitor music, and scrutinize television programs and the Internet for your children.

Loving Mother

*When you are a mother, you are never
really alone in your thoughts.*

*A mother always has to think twice,
once for herself and once for her child.*—
Sophia Loren, *Women and Beauty.*[3]

A truly good nurturing mother is one
who loves, cares, is gentle, and provides
nourishment—physically, mentally, emotionally, and spiritually for her
children.

Love your family and keep your home. Always be there to
love your children, and hold them when they need it. You are the
influencer. The influence a mother has on her children can make all
the difference as to what kind of persons your children will become.
What a mother writes on the hearts of her children, the world cannot
erase. Teach with strong conviction. A mother's corrective training
can lead a child to a better life. You need a sense of humor and
should be optimistic about the future. Laugher and joy changes any
atmosphere. Let it always be on your lips. Speak with wisdom, not
with nonsense and gossip. If you use wisdom, your children will listen
and understand. Never reveal your children's secrets, but be faithful
to keep what matters to them private. Be kind and teach by modeling
compassion. Children learn compassion and kindness when their
mother sets an example for them. True compassion is shown through
action, even to those who you may doubt.

Stand with your husband. Do everything you can to support your
husband in times of trouble.

Participate in and enforce family decisions.

Loving Children

Parents can only give good advice or put them on the right paths, but the final forming of a person's character lies in their own hands.—Anne Frank[4]

Children must regard and treat their parents with honor and respect. Children must hear and follow instruction. Wise children take note of and obey the instructions of their parents. When they do, they gain understanding. When children obey and are courteous to their parents, their lives will be long and happy. It is right to obey parents. Taking the wise counsel and obeying parents can keep children from harm. Siblings are an example to one another. Ephesians 6 says, "Children, obey your parents because you belong to the Lord for this is the right thing to do. Honor your father and mother."

This is the first commandment with a promise. If you honor your father and mother, things will go well for you, and you will have a long life on the earth.

Tips for a Nurturing Home

- Spend time together.
- Talk to one another.
- Keep a calm, interesting home.

CHAPTER 5

YOUR CHILD'S PLACE IN THE FAMILY MAKES A DIFFERENCE

Your children will become what you are; so be
what you want them to be.—David Bly[1]

Work, work, work. Do, do, do. Excel, excel, excel. All my life I pushed myself extremely hard. I was driven to excel in everything I did. Little did I know the driving force behind all that work was the middle-child syndrome. I wanted to be noticed, so I worked harder. I became an overachiever in everything I did because I craved attention. When it seemed my parents and siblings did not take notice, others spurred me on and gave me the congratulations and rewards for my accomplishments.

I remember the times of family conversations. The family members would give their input, and when it came to my turn, it seemed no one wanted to listen. I often thought, *when will what I have to say matter? Why is what I have to say not as important as what my siblings have to say?* I struggled for years to fit in, and my desire to be noticed subsided.

It is important that you help each of your children to see themselves as unique individuals and avoid comparisons with siblings or other people.

An only child grows up being the center of attention. Single children often mature faster because they spend a lot of time alone, with their parents, and their parents' friends. Single children generally get along well with older people and may prefer adult company and end up using adult language. Single children, having been the center of attention, sometimes have difficulty getting along or sharing with others. Single children are generally responsible, are often perfectionists, and seek attention. They can also be very independent and creative.

An oldest child, the firstborn, must relinquish all the attention. This can be hard for an oldest child. Many oldest children are often natural leaders. Their younger siblings often learn from them and look up to them. This often influences them to be more responsible and cooperative. Oldest children often become the movers and shakers. They like to have things under their control and want things their way. Oldest children are usually energetic, logical, ambitious, enterprising, and scholarly.

A second child often finds himself working hard to keep up with or even surpass his older sister or brother. It is impossible for the second child to have the parents' full attention, and so the challenge is to gain it. This sometimes results in a decision that he or she in every way will be different from the older child. What the older child likes, they hate. What the older child does, they refuse to do. This child can be a very diligent worker.

A middle child often feels squeezed between the older and younger children. Some middle children lack the self-confidence of only and older children. Fairness to middle children is most important. Middle children seek out and find ways to make it easier to get along with all kinds of people. Middle children can become problem children, as they misbehave to get attention. Middle children are generally fair. Middle children are generally flexible, diplomatic, and rebellious, seek attention, and are competitive.

A youngest child is quite willing to let others do for him or her. They can be charismatic and sociable or they can be domineering and demanding. Sometimes they use their charm to manipulate other people. Some youngest children give up too quickly. Others work hard to be more skillful than their brothers and sisters. They are usually charming and able to get their own way. They generally have a good sense of humor, are sensitive, secretive, and seek attention. Youngest children are often the risk takers and idealists.

Tip That Recognizes Each Family Member's Perspective

- When the family learns the effects of each family member's place, it will help everyone to view things and cooperate with one another from a different perspective.

CHAPTER 6

AGES AND STAGES OF DEVELOPMENT

You know children are growing up when they
start asking questions that have answers.
—John Plomp[1]

In order to know how best to respond and teach our children, it is important that we pay attention to the stages of development in our children.

From conception to eight years of age, our children are being grounded. They are experiencing the power of being, doing, and identifying. They are thinking about who they are, are attempting to find their own limits, are open and observant, and like to experiment. Questions fill their minds.

Children nine to twelve are at the stage of understanding. They are learning the power of being skillful and the effects of making mistakes. They find out what works and what does not. The moral values you have taught them begin to internalize. They have an insatiable need to know. They need guidance and constant clarification. They like to set goals. They crave unconditional love and acceptance.

Children thirteen to sixteen love to experience and share. It is a time of power, growth, and enlightenment. They seek fulfillment and attainment of their goals, and their beliefs and values are established.

They are developing a sense of direction. They pay attention to appropriate behaviors and cooperation. Responsibility, trust, and respect are important to them. Help them to develop problem-solving skills and give access to resources.

From seventeen to twenty, youth start living their experience. Most important is the power of acceptance. They transition from receiving to giving. They love to be mentored and to transfer those mentoring techniques to the next generation. They love recognition for their talents and abilities and love to be praised and encouraged. In turn, they will pass it on.

From twenty-one to thirty-two, it is time to demonstrate your experience. It is a time when individuals have power to conceive and create. They determine when it is right to reinforce or interfere and bring change. Commitment and faithfulness develop. Through gratefulness, humility, and personal truths, their lives begin to transform and take seriously and consider their effect on the next generation. Enjoy and encourage their joy in bringing change.

From thirty-three and older, it becomes a time of illumination. A lifestyle of living and releasing goodness and love; compassion, peace, and joy are important to them. They serve as catalysts and are constructive advisors. This is a time of building—building their own families, their own homes, their own careers. This generation loves to be an influence. Get and use their opinions. They can contribute much.

Tip for Responding to Your Child at Each Age Level

- Pay close attention to the stage of growth level for each child and respond accordingly.

CHAPTER 7

BUILD SELF-ESTEEM THROUGH
PRAISE FOR DOING AND BEING

Praise is like sunlight to the human spirit: We
cannot flower and grow without it
—Jess Lair[1]

Affirming words from moms and dads are like light switches.
Speak a word of affirmation at the right moment in a child's
life and it's like lighting up a whole roomful of possibilities
—Gary Smalley[2]

Good self-esteem is essential to a child's development. Self-esteem is the foundation of everything they do, everything they are, and is the foundation of their future! Each parent must realize that with great care, they direct their children and their household by doing what is right and just.

You must impress on the hearts of your children that you love them unconditionally. Talk to them when you sit together at home, when you drive around with them, when you lie down, and when you get up.

Everyone needs praise. It fuels and energizes our self-worth. Your children's feelings about themselves and their behavior greatly depend on receiving praise for being and doing. Praise makes them feel good and worthwhile and lets them know you are pleased. Parents usually find it easy to praise for doing, but praise for being takes a little more effort. Praise your children for being kind, polite, or honest. Parents can show praise in many ways with kind words, a smile, and a hug. Let praise and encouragement be a part of daily family life.

Express appreciation. Tell your children how much you appreciate them. Draw attention to their talents and good behaviors. Say things like, "The table looks great! Thank you for setting it so nicely." Or "I can always count on you to help me out. Thanks." Specific praise is a better guide for behavior.

Examples:

"I love the colors you picked for your drawing."

"I really liked how you shared your toys with your sister."

"You are doing so well at sounding out words when you read."

"I'm proud of how hard you tried at your dance contest today."

"You did such a great job memorizing your lines for the play."

"You must have studied really hard to get this grade on your test."

"I like your answer to this question."

"You did such careful work on your math homework, no wonder you got so many right!"

"I'm proud of how hard you worked on your project."

"I know this homework is hard for you, but if you continue working hard like you are, I know you can do it."

Tips to Enhance Good Self-Esteem in Your Children

- Kind yet firm correction best trains your children to obey you and to obey other authority.
- Consistent, loving correction helps children learn self-discipline.

- Giving up is not an option, even in the times when you may feel you have hopelessly ruined every chance for a loving relationship with your children.
- Consistent delivery of godly instruction and wisdom to your children is the key to effective parenting.
- Parental authority is abused and ineffective when you place irrational demands on your children. Let the discipline suit the age.
- When your children are more important than anything else in your life, it demonstrates true love and effective parenting.
- Compliment notes. You can put them with their lunch or on their bed.
- Write surprise sticky notes to your child.

Be Careful

Don't say anything demeaning or sarcastic. Even good-humored sarcasm is easily misunderstood by children, which can result in unintended hurt feelings.

Your children must know that their value is in who they truly are. Who they are is a mirror of you. Provide a positive reflection.

Chapter 8

Expressing Feelings Responsibly

Mankind are governed more by their feelings
than by reason.—Samuel Adams[1]

Feelings help make you who you are. They are our innermost experiences. They can be pleasant or unpleasant, mild or strong. You can keep them to yourself or share them with others. Our emotions usually push us into action. Help your children to understand their feelings by helping them put their emotions into words. Some children have very intense feelings and find it harder to control them. Others have to work hard even to know what their feelings are.

I will never forget the response of a seven-year-old in my pilot session of Nurturing Generation to Generation. It caused all of us to smile when we heard this little girl from a family of five express that she felt for the first time that her voice was heard. She was being listened to and was able to express her heart in family discussions. Her comment was, "I learned that I had a voice."

Children need a voice. Expressing and being responsible for the expression of feelings is the voice children need. Learning how is a lifelong process for children. Every family member's feelings are important and every member should share them.

Teach your children that they can feel what they want, but they must control what they do. Expressing feelings comfortably does not mean your children are free to explode at every emotional tremor. Children must learn to develop a comfortable balance between expressing and controlling feelings. Children must learn to keep a lid on their emotions, and at the same time, must feel that they can remove the lid in a safe environment.

In the days while I was teaching in the high school, there were oftentimes when teens would explode with emotion about things that had happened during the school day. I knew that in order for them to get control, it was important to ask questions about how they felt. They had to get these feelings in check before they could rightly determine what outcomes they would like to see or what future steps, if any, should be made. It was amazing what it did for them just to have someone consider their feelings.

Children pick up our attitude according to how we respond to their expressing their feelings. Your response determines whether your children think that you care to understand their feelings. When your children feel that their feelings are not worthwhile, they may begin to think they are not worthwhile, and then they might suppress or hide their feelings from you. Words like, "You are important to me, and your feelings are important to me" are more likely to get children to talk and work through their feelings.

Tips for Expressing Feelings Responsibly

- Take your children's feelings seriously and acknowledge how he/she is feeling.
- Never say, "It's not such a big deal" or "Why are you so upset about that?" Instead, help your children understand that on occasion, many people have similar feelings.

- Acknowledge your children's feelings and name them.
- Label the feeling, not the child.
- Give the reason for the feeling.
- Attempt to say why your children feel as they do. For example, say, "It looks like you're upset because you cannot go outside."
- Teach your child to express emotion in a healthy manner.
- Your children need to know that it is okay to express emotion in ways that are healthy and not hurtful to others.
- Try to set an example on how to handle frustration to your child.
- When you find yourself getting upset or frustrated, try saying things aloud like, "I'm sure I can get through this if I slow down and think about it."
- Teach your children how to put themselves in someone else's shoes.

Our feelings show in our faces. Think of the children's feeling song, "If you're happy and you know it, clap your hands; when you're angry and you know it, fold your arms; when you're sad and you know it, wipe your eyes; when you're scared and you know it, scream aloud."

Pay particular attention throughout the coming weeks and help your family express and work through their feelings positively.

CHAPTER 9

POSITIVE COMMUNICATION IN THE FAMILY

Communication is open and rules are flexible—the kind of atmosphere that is found in a nurturing family.—Virginia Satir[1]

Feelings of worth can flourish only in an atmosphere where individual differences are appreciated, mistakes are tolerated, communication is open, and rules are flexible—the kind of atmosphere that is found in a nurturing family.—Virginia Satir[2]

The best source of how families should communicate is found in scripture. We must learn to communicate wisely, speak from the heart, watch our mouths, build each other up, avoid foolish and stupid arguments, spare our words, keep a calm spirit, and allow the Holy Spirit to help us in our weaknesses. "But the things that proceed out of the mouth come from the heart and those define the man" (Matthew 15:18).

Be open in your communication. Think about when to talk, where to talk, what to talk about, and who should be involved. Set up the time and place that communication can take place. Having a serious discussion on the ride home from school or as soon as your children come in from school or right after you get home from work may not be the best of circumstances.

Rather than asking your child, "How was your day?" or "Did anything happen today that you might want to talk about?" you might say, "I take it all went well today." Your child then has the choice to tell you differently if he or she desires. When you bombard them with too many questions, they may feel on the spot, pressured, and may shut down.

What Is Non-Negotiable?

Establish and let your children know those things they cannot negotiate. You must be firm and consistent with what you allow or not allow. Children expect rules. Stick with your values and standards.

"Train them in the way they should go, and when they are old, they will not depart from it" (Proverbs 22:6). Never imply you might change your stand by saying things like, "I'll have to think about that."

Compromise in families means give and take for both parents and children. Expect something and be willing to give something. Children must consider the reasons for their parents' decisions. It may be that you value education and feel a part-time job may be distracting. You can agree to allow your teen to take a part-time job with a date for review of its effects on their schooling.

Be Specific

Family members must learn to be specific. "Your reading will likely improve if you sound out the words as you read," rather than saying, "I would like you to improve in your reading." "I want you to spend an hour practicing," rather than saying, "You need to spend more time practicing." A teen wanting an extended curfew should say, "I would like my curfew extended for an hour," rather than saying, "I need more freedom."

Practice what you preach to your children. Let it become a part of your nature. Thank family members for telling you how they feel. Let them know you appreciate it when they come to you with issues. Tell them you enjoy hearing about their day when good things happen so when bad things happen, they can come to you as well.

It is important that families enjoy their time together. Share fun things that each person can appreciate and takes an interest in. Enjoy outdoor activities and take vacations together. Brainstorm ideas together, and don't reject any ideas. Disagreements happen. Lingering resentment occurs when we don't get all comments and feelings out in the open at that time. Avoid blaming and accusatory language.

Follow principles of truth and love. Do not be contentious. When angry and in a conflict, both parties must stay respectful, talk about the real problem, look for areas of agreement, agree not to fight, wait and talk later. Families can cooperate to solve problems and have fun together. When there is a problem, you can choose to ignore it, use thoughtful listening, use an "I" message, give a choice, or work on solving it by exploring alternatives. When you talk with your child about a problem, use open-ended questions that begin with where, when, what, who, which, and how.

Tips for Fostering Conversation with Your Family

- Stay in synch with your family's level of conversation.
- Listen for the level of conversation your family is sharing with you and respond in a similar fashion.
- Some conversations can be casual and/or chatty.
- Other conversations may be more serious and/or emotional.
- Listen for conversations that your family is comfortable with and respond in a similar fashion.

- Some family members are more open than others are and will talk easily about themselves.

- Other family members are shy and may not talk at first, but once they feel comfortable, will become more talkative. These children often do best with brief conversations.

- Some family members prefer to vent a lot of pent-up feelings and may have minimal dialogue. For them, the best approach is just to listen and be the sounding board as they work it through.

- Humor may be a great tool in handling some difficult situations, but be careful of using humor during an emotionally charged conversation.

- Asking your teen this question, "Did anything unusual or different happen today that you would like to discuss?" allows him or her to set the agenda of a conversation.

CHAPTER 10

 LISTENING TO THE HEART

It is the province of knowledge to speak. And it
is the privilege of wisdom to listen.
—Oliver Wendell Holmes[1]

Most people never really listen. There is a distinction between merely hearing the words and listening for the message. Listening and acknowledging in families may seem simple, but most of the time we don't do it well. Family members must learn to listen to understand and reflect what they hear. "We are to be swift to hear and slow to speak" (James 1:19). Each must pay attention to each other's interest, not just their own. God listens to us with our issues—when we complain and when we are joyful. Families must do likewise.

Listening effectively is an important communication skill. How you listen is most significant. Listening in a way that demonstrates understanding and respect makes the difference. Children often feel like their parents do not hear them. Inside they are saying, "You just don't get it, do you?"

Sometimes your children just need to be heard and acknowledged before they become willing to consider an alternative to the position they presently hold.

Family members need to learn to listen as if they were standing in the other person's shoes, seeing through the other person's eyes, and listening through the other person's ears. Viewpoints may be different. You may not necessarily agree with the person, but as you listen, you understand from his or her perspective.

You practice active reflective listening when you listen attentively and repeat what you thought you heard. This helps to avoid misunderstandings because family members have to confirm that they do really understand what the other person has said. It tends to open up the conversation. When there is a conflict, family members often contradict one another, denying the other person's description of a situation. This tends to make people defensive, and they will either lash out or withdraw and say nothing more. However, when we feel that the other person is really attuned to our concerns and wants to listen, we are more likely to explain in detail what we feel and why. Now we can look at a solution.

Pay attention to the content and the feelings of what they are saying. For example, your child might say, "I don't like school. It isn't much fun." Talk about each aspect. Don't lecture them before they are finished talking and don't get angry. You may then learn how they really feel, or they may keep their feelings to themselves in the future. These types of conversation can dispel emotions.

Children get frustrated when you do not give your full attention. If you are unable to give your full attention at the time your child wants you to, let him or her know and set another time when you can focus. Make sure you get back to them.

Tips for Listening Well

- **Pay Attention.** Give your full attention. Prove you care by stopping all other activities. Don't pretend to listen while you formulate or plan your comeback. Rather than asking your child how was your day or did anything happen today that you might want to talk about, you might say, "I take it all went well today." Your child then has the choice to tell you differently if he or she desires. When you bombard them with too many questions, they may feel on the spot, pressured, and may shut down.

- **Respond.** Responses can be both verbal and nonverbal (nods, expressing interest) and prove you received the message. More importantly, prove it made an impression on you. Respond in ways that encourage the other person to share his/her reasons for feeling as they do.

- **Listen for Understanding.** Tell the person what you understand. When the message you receive is unclear or vague say, "Can you clarify that for me? Do you mean that? Are you saying . . . ?" This not only checks the accuracy of what you heard, it encourages the person to elaborate.

- **Paraphrase.** Prove your understanding by paraphrasing and using your own words to verbalize your understanding of what your child said. It helps your children to spot the flaws in their reasoning when they hear you play back without criticizing what they just said. It also helps identify areas of agreement so the areas of disagreement are not so magnified.

- **Reflect.** Reflecting what we hear gives us a chance to become aware of what is really going on below the surface. What are the feelings in a message? Reflective listening encourages the other person to become more aware of his or her feelings and express them more accurately. This helps to bring things into the open where they can be more readily resolved.

- **Respect.** Prove you take other's views seriously by choosing words and using a tone of voice that shows you are trying to imagine being where they are now.

- **Be Empathic and Nonjudgmental.** You can accept and be respectful of your children's viewpoints and their feelings without invalidating or giving up your own position.
- **Take Time to Practice Listening with Your Children or Friends**. See what a difference it makes. In your communications this week, try asking these kinds of questions: Are you saying? Do you mean? Can you clarify that for me? Tell me the whole story. I need to hear more about this. I'd like to hear your viewpoint. Would you like to talk about it? I gather you felt angry or frustrated or confused when . . . . Listen to the heart!

Things to Avoid When Listening

- Don't respond to just the meaning of the words, look for the feelings or intent beyond the words.
- Avoid looking at your watch or at other people or activities in the room.
- Be careful about crossing your arms and appearing closed or critical.
- Do not wait to promote your point of view.
- Do not interrupt.
- Watch your tone of voice, facial expressions, and posture.
- Avoid questions that hinder conversation. Do not try to solve the problem.
- Do not react to "push button" emotional words.

The enormous benefits of good listening are invaluable. Good listening takes effort, and every family can and should learn to do it. Listen with the mind and heart. Be genuinely interested in understanding the other's thinking and feelings. Be a ready listener and think before you speak.

Family members must learn to not only consider their own interest, but also consider the interests of others. We want others to listen to our issues when we complain, when we are joyful, and when we are broken. We want others to listen to our heart and respond with gentle words of love and understanding.

Chapter 11

Smoothing Out the Bumps in Family Life Problem Solving

A clever person solves a problem. A wise person avoids it.—Albert Einstein[1]

Do not be contentious. Families can cooperate to solve problems and have fun together. When there is a problem, you can choose to ignore it, use thoughtful listening, use an "I" message, give a choice, or work on solving it by exploring alternatives. When you talk with your child about a problem, use open-ended questions that begin with where, when, what, who, which, and how. When angry and in a conflict, both parties must stay respectful, talk about the real problem, look for areas of agreement, agree not to fight, or wait and talk later. Scriptures say, "Don't have anything to do with foolish and stupid arguments, because you know they produce quarrels. And the Lord's servant must not quarrel; instead, he must be kind to everyone, able to teach, not be resentful" *(*2 Timothy 2:22-25a).

Determine Who Owns the Problem

When there are problems with children, someone owns the problem. Sometimes the parent owns it. Sometimes the child owns it. Sometimes both the parent and child own it. The person who owns the problem is responsible for solving it. Help your children solve their own problems.

To decide who owns a problem, ask, whose rights are being disrespected? Could anybody get hurt? Is someone's property threatened? Is my child unable to take this responsibility? If the answer to any of the questions is yes, you—or you and your child—own the problem. If the answer to every question is no, your child owns the problem.

Listen to understand the problem, brainstorm ideas to solve it, discuss possible solutions, and then choose a solution (whoever owns the problem gets to pick). If dually owned, both pick. It helps to review the positive and negatives of each option, and then select the option that generates the most positive or least negative feelings. Once you have selected an option, set a time, perhaps the following week, to discuss whether the idea is working.

Problem Solving with "I" Messages

"I" messages let people know what we are thinking. "I" messages help to facilitate constructive dialogue in problem solving. "I" messages help to ease tension and conflict, reduce defensiveness, better prepare the listener for feedback, foster honest communication, and assist in defining the problem you are having or the message you want to send.

Here is a scenario for you. It's Friday morning and thirteen-year-old Rebecca walks into the kitchen. She stands by the counter and waits for her mom to notice her. Mom looks up from the paper. She sees Rebecca and feels annoyed. Mom says, "Rebecca, you can't go to school in that top. I can see your belly button!" Rebecca says, "This is Kay's shirt, and she wears it all the time. I think it looks nice!" "Go and change," Mom says. Rebecca sighs, "Oh, all right."

Five minutes later, Rebecca is back. Mom takes one look at her and rolls her eyes. "You can't wear those ripped jeans! My goodness, Rebecca, why won't you put on something decent?" Rebecca says, "Okay, okay." She hurries off and returns wearing a pair of clean jeans and a blouse. Mom says, "That's better."

Rebecca eats a bowl of cereal. She goes back to the bedroom for her books. When she returns to the kitchen, Mom sees that Rebecca has put on eye shadow. Mom sighs and says, "Now, look at you! That's way too much eye shadow!" Mom takes a tissue and wipes off some of the eye makeup.

How Can "I" Messages Be Used by Mom and Rebecca?

Mom can express her true feelings to Rebecca, "It really bothers me when you wear outfits that show your belly button. I don't believe you want to draw attention to who you are on the outside rather than who you are inside. What I would like is for you to wear an outfit that reflects that person."

As for the ripped jeans, Mom can ignore the holes. It is important that Mom comment positively on Rebecca's final selection. As for the eye shadow, Mom can take another opportunity to show Rebecca how to wear eye makeup appropriately.

Rebecca, rather than standing at the kitchen counter awaiting her mom's attention, should ask her mom what she thinks of her outfit. Mom, at that point, can be honest with her about what she thinks. Rebecca, though she may not be saying the words aloud, is asking for her mom's opinion. At Mom's response, Rebecca could say, "It really bothers me when you look at me like that. Just give me an order to change my outfit. What I would like is for you to tell me why you think something is inappropriate and give me assistance with my choices." What an awesome opportunity for Mom and Rebecca.

Rather than saying things like, "You broke your promise," it would be better to say, "I was so disappointed when . . . ."

When you are attempting to solve a problem, there is a strong tendency to blame the problem on the other person. "I" messages simply state a problem without blame. This makes it easier for the other side to help solve the problem without having to admit that they were wrong. "You" messages suggest blame and encourage the other person to deny wrongdoing or to blame back. For example, if you say, "You broke your promise," the answer is likely to be, "No, I didn't," which sets you up for a lengthy argument, or "Well, you did, too," which also continues the conflict.

"I" messages are a key part of being respectful.

Once you state your "I" message, be prepared to use your active listening skills. As you listen to your child's perceptions and needs, you will often find the keys to reaching a solution that will satisfy both of you.

Tips for Resolving Problems

- Listen to understand. It is necessary to resolving problems.
- Whoever owns the problem is responsible to choose the solution to the problem.
- "I" messages remove blame and generally produce results that are more positive.

CHAPTER 12

FAMILY DECISION MAKING

Decision is a sharp knife that cuts clean and straight;
indecision is a dull one that hacks and tears and leaves
ragged edges behind it.—Gordon Graham[1]

Decisions surround us every day. Our lives are orientated around loving, serving, and our decision-making should reflect that. Family members have different thoughts, feelings, and ideas that can make decision-making challenging. The ability to make good and wise decisions is a skill that parents help children to learn and improve upon.

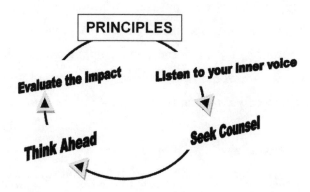

Follow wise principles of truth, love, and do not be contentious. Shape decisions based on wise principles.

Listen to your inner voice as you think through decisions. Take the time to think through and meditate, read related information, journals, or talk with others.

Seek Counsel. Find a trusted and wise person to consult. You must help your children to identify these people in advance, so if they feel uncomfortable talking with you they can go to that person.

Think Ahead. Consider the outcome of each alternative you consider. What will be the result of each choice? How will each choice influence those involved in your decision? Will your decision affect anyone else besides them? Consider the consequences of your decisions. Teach your child to think ahead and take responsibility for his or her decisions and the potential outcomes before they are made.

Evaluate the Effect. Teach your children to set a time for reconsideration of the decision they made. If the results are not what they hoped for, they can make another decision. Make them aware that sometimes the consequences of some decisions cannot be reversed, but they can move you forward to make wiser choices in the future.

Our choices affect us and other members of our family. Do you make your decisions on impulse, emotions, feelings, thought and research, or does your upbringing, previous experience, or the media influence you? Let your decision-making motto be, "I will let love abound more and more in knowledge and depth of insight so that I may be able to discern what is best" (Philippians 1:9).

Children learn best by how we make decisions. Help them to learn how to make wise decisions by referring to old stories of honesty, integrity, character, work ethic, sexual behavior and its consequences, substance abuse, etc. Children are inclined to be impulsive. They will not learn entirely on their own. They need your help. Live it and share yours and other stories with them.

Jeremy is sixteen years old. He wants a car, so he gets a part-time job. His job will pay for insurance and gas, but not expensive repairs. Jeremy's parents are glad he is willing to work for something he wants, but they worry that he won't be able to afford repairs on a junker. They wish he had saved a bit more money for a better car. So they give their son a choice.

He may buy the junker. If he does, Jeremy must pay for all repairs. If the car breaks down, he'll share the family car with his parents or find other rides.

Jeremy decides to buy the junker and before long, things go wrong. The repairs are expensive and soon Jeremy can't even drive it. He has to get rides with friends and use the family car. His parents respect his decision. They don't say, "We told you so," and they don't give Jeremy help to pay for his car expenses.

Jeremy learned that he is responsible for his decisions. His parents love and respect him, and in the future, he must act more responsibly.

Once your child makes a decision, hold him or her responsible. For example, if he or she chooses to play basketball, make them continue until the end of the season. If they choose to play an instrument, they must continue until the year's end. Do not bail them out. Future good decision making is best learned from the results of bad decision making. Review with them the helpful hints of halt, consider, evaluation, and action.

Discuss with your children any bad decisions they have made. Help them to judge what they can learn for the future. Be willing to share with them the bad choices you have made and the consequences that came with those choices. How did it help you? You can also help your children by presenting them with hypothetical situations, such as a moral dilemma about lying to a friend.

Good decision makers are made. When you take your children to a restaurant, give them the amount they can spend before you enter the building. When you take them to buy new shoes, clothes, etc., give them the limit you will contribute. Give them a list of activities in which they can participate, and allow them to choose one or two, and make them stick to their choice.

Tips for Decision Making

- Halt. How does this decision help? Can I achieve my goal with this decision?
- Consider. Do I have other options? What other information do I need?
- Evaluate. Which choices are helpful? Which choices are hurtful? What are the risks?
- Act. What steps do I need to take? When will I take what steps?
- Self-congratulations. Have I congratulated myself or shared my accomplishment with someone?

Chapter 13

Discipline That Makes
a Difference

*Discipline doesn't break a child's spirit half as often
as the lack of it breaks a parent's heart.*
—Author unknown[1]

Discipline is about instruction. It means to teach. There is an old saying, "Spare the rod, spoil the child." Why not let that rod be like the rod that shepherds use to discipline their sheep. Parents are the shepherds of protection, guidance, care, and they nurture as we guide our children into adulthood. Shepherds use their rod to send wandering sheep scurrying back to the flock, ward off animals or intruders, account for each sheep, and part the wool to examine for disease, wounds, or defects. Do not abandon your children to their own devices and limited experiences. You be their guide.

Discipline to a child should not mean punishment. Think of each conflict as an opportunity to guide and direct your child about what is right or wrong. Every situation is an opportunity to help show your child the appropriate reaction. Instead of punishing a child for misbehaving, think in terms of teaching him to behave. Remember, the behavior needs fixing, not your child.

One day, my child had to stay home for unruly behavior at school. I decided to keep the order of the school day by starting with prayer and scripture reading. We prayed about his inappropriate behavior and then asked the Lord to deal with his heart. My son had to read the scripture. Without thought or prompting, he opened to Psalms 101:2 that said, "I will behave myself wisely and walk in a perfect way." God sent his word to my son. He knew what he had to do. Behaving wisely would help him avoid negative consequences in the future.

The rod in every mother or father's hand is the words they speak. You must be wise, kind, and yet firm in your correction. Being consistent in delivering wise, loving correction helps children to learn self-discipline. Physical and emotional punishment can cause harm. Negative words can actually harm children more. Emotional abuse is often very subtle. Giving up is not an option, even when you begin to wonder if you have ruined every chance for a loving relationship with your children.

It has been said that 90 percent of parents spank at least occasionally. It is not that spanking is completely wrong, but we must check our motivation. Parents say they spank because it works, it's quick, it establishes the parent as the authority figure, and it catches the child's attention.[2] Ask yourself, does the behavior ever return, or does it only work in the short-term? Spanking ought to be the discipline of last choice after all else has failed, and never spank out of anger.

If your child is misbehaving and verbal discipline is not working, consider there may be an outside influence affecting his or her behavior. Sometimes things such as a friend, lack of sleep or food, television, or even some underlying illness may be influencing the child's behavior. This discipline problem may quickly disappear with the removal of the influence.

There are many successful ways to manage a child's behavior. Count to ten and think. Ask yourself, "What do I really want to accomplish here?" Play music. Remember how much you love your child and think about the best way to show that to your child. Be constructive and non-hurtful. You and your child will feel better.

Tips for Disciplining Your Children

Things to Avoid

- *Apologizing for having to discipline.* You are actually teaching your child a lesson in how to behave. Therefore, taking away the punishment five minutes after you instituted it only serves to cause your child to think either you are angry or the behavior was not very bad.

- *Hesitating when you come up with a consequence.* Once you come up with a consequence for your child when he has misbehaved, stick to it or all of your credibility goes out the window in a flash. Sounding indecisive only teaches your child that the consequence is questionable. For example, don't ask— tell. "You will not be watching any TV this evening," not "You will not be any watching TV this evening, okay."

- *Applying the same discipline strategy to all of your children.* What works for one child may not work for all of them. Different consequences lead to different outcomes depending on the child's age, so try to pick whatever consequences will work best for each child. Make sure the consequence is age and temperament appropriate.

- *Responding in an overly emotional way.* Losing your cool can cause you to make poor discipline decisions. It will be hard, but you must stay calm, cool, and collected. Take a deep breath—no screaming or shouting. This will give you time to come up with an appropriate discipline. There's nothing wrong with saying, "I'm too angry to deal with this now. We'll talk about it later."

- *Allowing too long a delay between the inappropriate behavior and the discipline.* You want your child to remember exactly why you are disciplining him. If you wait too long, he may not remember the inappropriate behavior. Only when you are too angry to make a rational decision, or when you are likely to cause undue embarrassment to your child, should you delay.

- *Allowing the punishment to last too long.* Making the punishment last too long or taking away too many privileges at a time can cause a child to abandon all hope and lose all incentive to behave. It can lead to an all-out rebellion; not only that, but you lose some of your discipline options for that period.

- *Looking the other way when there is inappropriate behavior.* Misbehavior will continue when you give in. For example, when you do the dirty dishes they were supposed to do, when you clean their rooms, and when you put their dirty clothes in the hamper, you will be stuck doing those things. Children must learn to take responsibility and suffer the consequences for their misbehavior.

Alternatives to Punishment

- *Change the environment.* It may be easier to change your child's environment. For example, if your child repeatedly breaks your glass dishes, give him plastic dishes.

- *Offer an acceptable alternative.* Your child can be satisfied with another choice. If you do not want your child to jump on the bed, don't just say, "You can't do that." Find something else that springs.

- *Model an appropriate behavior.* If your child puts the entire roll of tissue in the toilet, show him how to tear off two or three sheets of paper. Words alone are not always enough.

- *Choices empower, commands cause power struggles.* Help your child to make a decision. It empowers him. When you command, it invites a power struggle. For example, ask, "Would you like to wear your blue jeans or a pair of shorts today?"

- *Concessions in small doses often help.* You can say, "You can stay up until you finish reading that chapter, then it is lights out."

- *Prepare for possible difficulties.* You are expecting guests for dinner. Discuss and practice appropriate behavior. Be specific. How should the child greet the guests? Teach him that when someone passes him something at the table say, "Thank you."

- *Let natural consequences occur.* Someone steps on your child's favorite toy and now it is broken. The child learns that if toys aren't put away, they may get broken. Never create an artificial consequence.

- *Your feelings count.* Let children know how their behavior affects you. For example, "I get so tired of trying to keep dinner warm."

- *Hold your child.* Pent-up feelings are often released in the healing tears that flow as you hold and support your child in a loving way.

- *Take action when necessary.* If your child insists on riding his bike in the street, allow bike riding only when you are watching. Explain the dangers.

- *Take your child out of the situation.* Once removed, take this time to listen, share feelings, hold, and talk about how to resolve the conflict.
- *Be playful.* Change what might be a difficult time into a fun time. For example, during mealtime, let the child give you a teaspoon of vegetables, and then you give the child some vegetables.
- *Defuse the situation with laughter.* Laughter helps resolve anger and feelings of powerlessness. If your child is mad at you, invite him to express his anger in a playful pillow fight with you. Play your part by surrendering dramatically.
- *Negotiate.* If your child wants to go out with his friend on Friday, which may be room-cleaning night, reach an agreement that on Sunday he must clean his room by 3:00 p.m.
- *Appropriate expectations.* Learn to accept your children as they are. At varying stages in life, some children have intense feelings and needs; some are naturally loud, some are curious, some are messy, some are strong willed, some are impatient, some are full of energy, some are demanding, some are creative, and some are forgetful, fearful, or even self-centered.

When disciplining your child, look for deep-seated needs. Does your child require attention? You might tickle the child who is whining. Explain your reasons. You might say, "We always drink our juice in the kitchen so the carpet doesn't get sticky and dirty." Look for underlying feelings. When your child snatches a toy, encourage him to express his anger in a way that does not cause harm. Emphasize the positives.

Be smart in your discipline. If what you're doing isn't working, <u>find a more effective way to handle the problem</u>. It is much easier to change your approach than it is to change your child. Ask yourself, "What can I do differently that will inspire a better reaction from my child?" Nothing is as frustrating or less productive as having <u>a showdown</u> with your child. Solicit your child's help for a solution to a problem.

Younger children learn best by doing what they see you do. Therefore, model good behavior, show good manners, look them in the eyes when you talk to them, and always speak in a normal, respectful tone. Older children respond better to having privileges removed. Make sure it is a decision you can live with, reinforce, and make sure they fully understand why you removed the privilege. Stick to your decisions.

Be sure your anger doesn't influence your discipline. If you need one, give yourself a cooling off period before confronting your child.

Things to Consider When Spanking Your Children

It can teach children that hitting is okay. (How many times have you seen your children spank their doll or hit one another? Where did they learn that?)

- It can lead to injury or abuse.
- It can lead to not doing certain things in your presence, but doesn't teach them proper behavior.
- It can confuse young children who don't yet connect their actions to the punishment.
- It can make the parent seem out of control.
- It can communicate to children that a loving relationship includes violence.

Chapter 14

Family Cooperation

If you want children to keep their feet on the ground,
put some responsibility on their shoulders.
—Abigail Van Bure[1]

Family Rules

Family rules promote and reinforce cooperative behavior. Determine family rules together. "Through wisdom a house is built, and by understanding it is established. By knowledge, the rooms are filled with all precious and pleasant riches" (Proverbs 23:3-4).

Everyone in the family should participate in making family rules. Children will be much more likely to respect decisions and rules that they helped create. Family ground rules involve dos and don'ts that all family members need to follow. For every *don't* rule, there must be a *do* rule. Rules have to be fair, clear, specific, reasonable, and possible. Teach your children the reasons behind family rules. Teach your children future skills—laundry, cooking, balanced meals, money management, time management, etc. Teach spiritual development— praying together, etc. Teach responsibility through chores, etc. Set rules to help them take care of themselves, avoid dangerous situations, and to respect themselves and others.

Discuss how different families have different rules. Let your children know that in different houses and in different countries, families may have different rules. In your family, your child follows your family's rules. Discuss your rules and expectations in advance.

Three Kinds of Family Rules

Ground Rules

Everyone follows these rules, no matter what. Rules about politeness and not hurting others are examples of ground rules. They apply to the whole family.

Situation Rules

Rules for traveling in the car, visiting at another person's house, and using the computer are rules that might be situation rules.

Changing Rules

As children grow older, rules about privacy might become more important. Curfews might change. At this time, you might want to revise important rules. Make sure everyone is aware.

Don't make too many rules because you might not remember or enforce them all consistently. Respect children's rights, such as the right to privacy, within the family rules. Don't make any rules you do not intend to enforce. Rules without consequences have no meaning for children, so set rules you know you can and will enforce. Don't impose harsh or unexpected new punishments. Stick to consequences that have been set ahead of time. Make age-appropriate consequences. Praise children when they follow the rules. Positive reinforcement helps them develop self-confidence and trust in their own judgment. Talk about needed changes in the rules.

Tips for Setting up Family Rules

- Decide what rules are givens and what are negotiable.
- Gather family members together and brainstorm a list of family rules. For example, "We speak quietly with one another," "We put others first," "We always tell the truth," and so on.
- Write the rules down and make sure everyone knows them.
- Let younger children illustrate on a poster using stick figures or magazine cutouts.
- Post rules in a prominent place in your home. (e.g., on the refrigerator)
- Discuss how rules protect health, safety, and rights.
- Let children know you love them too much to let them take dangerous risks or get into trouble.
- Seek support from other adults whose ability to parent you respect.
- Getting teens/children to cooperate requires parents to show respect.
- Define givens, but negotiate other limits.
- Choose limits that are age appropriate (fewer rules with older children).
- Give everyone a chance to discuss the fairness of the rules.

CHAPTER 15

WHEN YOUR CHILD MISBEHAVES

To become emotionally mature, children must learn from
failure and face the consequences of their poor choices.
—Jacquie McTaggart[1]

Consequences are what children can expect when rules are or are
not followed. Consequences show respect for all, are about and fit the
misbehavior, are about the future, and are firm and friendly. Make sure
everyone understands the consequences for breaking the rules. Follow
through with the consequences. Children need to know that rules are
enforced.

Consequences follow when your child breaks a rule or does
something wrong. When behavior needs correcting, refer to the rules
to reinforce the behavior that doesn't meet your family's standards and
help them understand that they are responsible for their misbehavior—
it's against the rules (not just someone having a bad day). Keep your
voice in a normal tone and your emotions under control. When you
yell, order, or threaten, it shifts focus from the child's behavior to your
behavior. Try to understand what happened and what your child was
thinking and feeling. If you are emotional or upset, set a future time to
discuss consequences (e.g., next day after school).

Be sure that anger doesn't influence your discipline. If you need one, give yourself a cooling-off period before confronting your child about rule breaking.

Remember, persistence is the name of the game!

Tips for Using Consequences

- Determine the consequence. Involve children in responsibility for poor choices.
- Fit the consequence to the behavior. (e.g., If rude to a sibling, do a chore for that sibling, or if you steal from a sibling, return the item, and pay for any damages.)
- Fit the consequence to your child's development level (e.g., don't require a five-year-old to write, "I will not lie" one hundred times).
- Don't negotiate, set consequences.
- Be consistent.
- Don't wait.
- Carry out the consequence as immediately as convenient.
- Make sure all necessary parties are aware of the consequences—spouse, teacher, babysitter, grandparents—and anyone who knows of your agreed to specific behaviors.

CHAPTER 16

RESPONSIBILITY AND RESPECT IN YOUR HOUSEHOLD

If you want children to keep their feet on the ground,
put some responsibility on their shoulders.
—Abigail Van Bure[1]

Children learn by taking responsibility for their appropriate and inappropriate behavior. Hold them accountable for their actions. Show them the proper way to handle responsibility. Don't threaten. Don't change your position on an issue because of a threat. When forced to respond immediately, briefly say what you expect to happen. Tell your child that you love him and are doing what you believe is best for him.

Respect is earned. Demanding or forcing respect does not result in the kind of response you might want. Respect your children. Discipline in private. Stay calm. Remain neutral. Model respect, reasonableness, and flexibility. Respect means many different things. On a practical level, it seems to include taking someone's feelings, needs, thoughts, ideas, wishes, and preferences into consideration.

Ask them how they feel. "How would you feel if . . ." Validate their feelings. "It sounds like you feel . . ." Empathize with them. "I can see why you feel that way . . ." Seek understanding of their feelings. "Help me to understand why you feel . . ." Consider their feelings in final decisions. "Given what you have said, "Let's . . ." And finally, ask, "How do you feel about that?"

For this process to work efficiently, people must be aware of their own feelings. (i.e., know how they feel, must be able to express their feelings, must know how to listen, not be judgmental or defensive, must know how to validate feelings of others, must believe that feelings have value, and they must believe that feelings matter.)

Specific Ways to Show Respect

Children are human beings and deserve respect as a person. Parents should find positive ways to help their children grow up to be respectful and responsible adults. Establish an atmosphere where your children feel that you care for them, enjoy being with them, and respect them by taking their feelings, interests, and ideas into account.

There are countless forms of subtle respect or disrespect. Showing respect means not yelling, calling names, being sarcastic, or otherwise speaking to one another in ways you would want to be spoken to. Disrespect is not taking that person's feelings, needs, and thoughts into consideration.

Chores

Give children age-appropriate chores—one to three chores per child. It teaches them responsibility. Just like us, children don't like chores. I remember one of my sister's children telling his mom that he knew why she had children—to do all the things she didn't want to do. Have a chore, like yard cleanup that the whole family can complete together. It makes major chores more fun and gives parents a chance to set an example.

Children learn by taking responsibility for their appropriate and inappropriate behavior. Hold them accountable for their actions. Show the proper way to handle responsibility. Don't threaten. Don't change your position on an issue because of a threat. When forced to respond immediately, briefly say what you expect to happen. Tell your child that you are doing what you believe is best for him. Because you love him, you cannot change your position.

Family Meetings

Family meetings can make a difference in how your household cooperates. Focus on the positive. Family meetings are not only gripe sessions. Take time to eat popcorn, sing, show off, and enjoy your family. Teach your children how to come to specific solutions.

Family meetings can be a time to coordinate the running of the household. Schedule car pools and rides, chores, special events, vacations, and holiday planning. Announce family decisions, discuss serious family issues, come up with new ideas, and problem solve issues, recognize and celebrate each family member's biggest accomplishments since the last family meeting, and relax with one another—eat, drink, and be merry!

Plan the family meeting ahead of time, far enough ahead so everyone can be there. Make sure every family member has the specific date on his/her calendar. Set up the agenda in advance so that everybody can have input and to avoid squabbles. Post an agenda suggestion list in the kitchen. Keep family meetings to thirty minutes. Take turns planning and facilitating the meetings.

You could take the family meeting times to tell your children stories of when you were their age, share fun memories, major events, embarrassing or funny experiences, what you did after school, your struggles, etc. Use old photos to share stories and learning experiences about when you were growing up, especially when you were their age.

Have time set aside with your children to discuss their plans and goals—high school activities, dating, college, marriage, career, etc. Both parents should be included in the conversation. Express genuine interest in their feelings, thoughts, interests, friends, and worries.

Start family traditions. Traditions provide children with an important sense of belonging. They don't have to be elaborate in order to be fun or memorable. In my family, Sunday breakfast together in a household of fourteen was a challenge. We all planned and looked forward to Sundays. My father often surprised us by getting up early and making donuts. I maintained that early morning Sunday breakfast tradition with my family.

Family Safety Rules

Family meetings are the ideal place for discussing rules for family safety. Establishing a system of family rules about personal safety can be a good way to teach children to distinguish between safe and non-safe situations. By adopting rules about personal safety, you can teach good habits through reinforcement and repetition without generating excessive fear.

Develop a family code word. If someone other than a parent is going to pick up a child unexpectedly, that person should repeat the code word first before the child agrees to leave. The code word should remain a secret and be changed when others learn of it.

Schools have specific rules about emergency pick-ups. Please make sure you are aware of those rules and provide the school with the information needed.

Tips for Inside and Outside Rules

Inside Rules

- Your children should know their complete home address, telephone number (including area code), and their parents' first and last names.
- You should teach your children never to reveal any personal (their name, school, age, etc.) or family information over the phone or on the Internet unless a parent has given permission.
- If your children are home alone and answer a phone call, they should say, "She can't come to the phone right now." They should take a message or tell the caller to try later. Don't make excuses, they sound phony.
- It is okay not to answer the phone or to work out a code (ring twice, hang up, call again) so you can check on a child who is home alone.
- Your children are old enough to answer the door when they are old enough to check the identity of the person at the door without opening it.
- Your children should help you make sure the doors that should be locked are locked.
- Your children should avoid Internet chat rooms.

Outside Rules

- Establish a system of accountability.
- Avoid construction sites, dark streets, and alleyways.

- Learn the full names of your children's friends, their parents' names, addresses, and phone numbers. Check to verify the accuracy if you get the information from your kids.
- When your child is at a friend's home, who else is present? Parents? Older kids? Other neighbors? No one? Check it out.
- Know your children's routes to and from school, play, and errands. Insist they stick to the same route—no shortcuts! If you have to look for them, you will know where to begin.
- Your children should be taught never to go anywhere with anyone without your permission. This includes getting permission a second time if plans change and calling to check before going from one friend's home to another location.
- Your children should never play in isolated areas of parks or playgrounds and should avoid public restrooms.
- Teach your children alternatives. If they are bothered or followed on the playground, should they walk to a friend's home, school, or store? Where should they go? Walk these common routes with your children and look for choices. Can they go back into the school, in a store or business (kids are reluctant to enter a strange store or business unless given permission), into a fire station or approach someone doing yard work?
- Knocking on the door of a stranger is a last resort. If they have no other choice, they should look for a house with a light on (at night) or toys in the yard (if possible), and ask the homeowner to "Please call the police, someone is bothering me," but not go inside the house.
- A child's best defense is his/her voice and legs. Teach them to run away from someone who is bothering them while yelling

to attract as much attention as possible. Have them practice yelling!

- Teach your children not to approach drivers in cars that stop and ask for help. If the car follows them or the driver gets out, the child should run away and yell.

- Teach your children that a stranger is someone who they do not know. A friend of parents, a friend of the child's friend or a neighbor can be a stranger. A stranger can be a good guy or a bad guy.

- Some bad guys act nice and are friendly. Some bad guys play tricks on kids. Typical bad guy tricks include bribes (money, toys, games, or promises of those things), lies (your mom told me to pick you up at school), requests for help (my puppy ran away, can you help me find him?), or threats (if you don't come with me, I'll hurt your mom).

- Teach kids that a bad guy is someone who asks them to violate family rules. (e.g., someone who says you don't need permission to accompany me.)

Conclusion

As noted in my introduction, I used the material in this book to pilot Nurturing Generation to Generation in Atlanta, Georgia. We have had some successful family breakthroughs—helping teens overcome contemplation of suicide, reconsideration of a marriage about to break up, a single mom about to give up on a teenage son. Families repeatedly told us that we must continue our efforts because it was so effective in stabilizing their homes. In our pilot program, we trained nineteen facilitators and serviced eighteen families.

The words of one participant best expressed a changed life in their families. "Before the Nurturing Generation to Generation Program, we always struggled with discipline. I was always yelling at the children. It was my way or no way. Our house was amuck; I was always stressed because we rarely held the children or ourselves accountable for things that were supposed to be done. Cameron and Candace were being rebellious. Cameron would yell back at me. I felt like even Candace, as young as she was, was learning how to manipulate to get her way.

"I have learned through this program that there are other ways to address what seem to be almost impossible situations. The nurturing a generation program has taught our family to be more effective communicators. We have learned to set clear rules and the importance of writing them down. We have learned the importance of accountability. We have learned what it means to be a family. We feel that no matter what, our nurturing a generation family will always be there for us, to mentor, give words of encouragement, and just be a positive force for us in our journey. We would like to thank everyone who had a part in this inspiration. It has truly been a blessing for our family."

One of the families wrote up and read at a meeting a twelve-covenant commitment that they made between themselves. Their words moved us as we listened to parents and children (seven, ten, twelve, and fourteen) of another family who shared how they are now listening, respecting, considering, and responding to one another in a more positive manner. Life is not the same in this household, as they have embraced and applied the teaching.

Other families expressed that they too are grateful that someone cared enough to take time with them so that they could learn a better way. Many family members shared the effectiveness of such teaching.

Comments from one of the facilitators, "I wanted to share just a brief thought in the way of testimony concerning the nurturing program. I have received a tremendous amount of information, which has helped to dispel some of the myths and wives tales that baby boomers passed down to us. That was so powerful and freed me from some old thinking. The real testimony for me is that I am very hopeful at this point. With the situation seeming somewhat bleak for the family, I feel and sense hope. When I see the young people, not just coming on Friday, but also wanting to come, it makes it all worthwhile. During the week, if I see some of them, they will give me reports or even ask how I'm doing, and it lets me know they are receiving something from the program. I believe they will take this program and will pass it on. I feel very hopeful."

Another facilitator commented on how the relationship between she and her father was restored using the tools provided.

As you apply the tools given in this book, you too, will see changes in your family. Expect the flow of love to increase, expect that family members will begin to express their feelings openly and responsibly, expect conversations to be more positive, expect that family members will listen better, expect to solve problems more responsibly and respectfully, and expect improved family cooperation.

About the Author

I grew up in a family of fourteen brothers and sisters. There were good times and bad times, times of abundance, and times of lack. However, there was one thing we never lacked—we all knew we were valued and loved. My parents set the standards by which we would live, and they spent countless hours teaching us to honor and serve one another.

Our home was a place where love abounded. As if fourteen children were not enough, my parents extended their love to many young people whose lives were in shambles. We took in foster children, children from broken homes, children who had problems in their homes, and children who didn't know what family was all about. As these young people periodically came to live with us, the whole family embraced them until the inner healing that those young people needed took place. Further, as I witnessed the healing that was taking place in these children, little did I know that a seed of destiny was being sown deep within me.

As the years passed, I felt the need to learn how people think and how they could best cooperate. My studies in psychology and sociology prepared me with knowledge and insight into the mind and social environment. That knowledge was not enough. My heart was overtaken with desire to help the generations realize their potential and recognize how positive parenting could help them get there. Parental love and effective communication would see them through.

This prompted me to enter the teaching profession, which provided opportunities for me to work with parents and children. I was amazed at the number of times that youth and parents came to me seeking assistance to help them build a bridge of positive communication.

After fifteen years in the field of education, I began to work with those who had lost touch with their families. I listened to the tales of woe, of neglect, of lack, and of feelings of desperation. They needed to feel loved and to have someone listen to their hearts. I vividly remember those times, and I could feel the brokenness of hurting hearts.

I eventually became staff pastor at my church. I worked with the young, teens, young adults, and parents. I was seized with an overwhelming awareness of the need, significance, and importance of effective communication in the home. The young were looking for guidance in how they should act, the teens needed direction in how to handle themselves, and the young adults were seeking fulfillment as they looked forward to the challenges of their future. At each step, parents often struggled with what to do or not do in helping their children develop and move forward in life.

These experiences, along with my visit to a county juvenile delinquency court where I heard young people and parents cry out for help in their communication processes, led to the development and piloting of the Nurturing Generation to Generation, a family program in Atlanta, Georgia. Results were astounding. Family members reported that the tools they had been given had helped them to dramatically change the dynamics in their home. Bridges of love and acceptance, positive communication, fair and right discipline and consequences, and family cooperation were established in their homes. The facilitators and I realized that if the family participated in a program that would open the doors to better and more appropriate communication, their direction would change.

My lifelong experience, the challenges I have faced, and the families I have helped inspired this book, which I believe will help you to learn to establish and practice positive experiences within your home. A never-ending bridge can be built between the generations.

REFERENCES

Chapter 1

1. Burrows, Eva (2008). *QuoteLucy.com*, Lucy Media, Quote, Quotation 203555, accessed April 12, 2013.
2. Baumrind, D. (1991). The influence of Parenting Style on Adolescent Competence and Substance Use, *Journal of Early Adolescence, 11(1)*, 56-95.
3. Damon, W. (Ed.). (1989) *Child Development Today and Tomorrow*. San Francisco, CA, Jossey-Bass, 137-154.
4. Coats, Carolyn (1994). Living Life Fully, accessed August 12, 2012, *Things Your Dad Always Told You But You Didn't Want to Hear, Nelson edition, in English,* http://www.livinglifefully. com/rolemodels.html.

Chapter 2

1. Robbins, Tony. Quote from KC King *Philosiblog.com*, August 31, 2012, accessed June 12, 2013, http://www.brainyquote. com/quotes/quotes/t/tonyrobbin147775.html.
2. Iannelli, Vincent, M.D., *Parenting Styles*, Updated December 13, 2004, accessed December 8, 2013, http://pediatrics.about. com/od/infantparentingtips/a/04_pntg_styles.html.

Chapter 3

1. Koop, C. Everett, *Goodreads Quotes,* accessed April 12, 2012, *http://www.goodreads.com/quotes/185539.*

Chapter 4

1. Rohn, Jim. *Searchquotes.com, Family Loyalty Quotes,* accessed June 6, 2013, http://www.searchquotes.com/quotation/su/321150.
2. Pittman, Frank. *Man Enough,* accessed June 6, 2013, www.goodreads.com/author/quotes/341540.
3. Loren, Sophia. Inspirational Quotes on Mothers' Day by, Women and Beauty, *Society for the Confluence of Festivals in India, B-30,* Kendriya Vihar, sector 51, NOIDA, UP-201301, India.
4. Frank, Anne. *Education.com Magazine, Parenting and Families,* accessed December 8, 2013, http://www.education.com/magazine/article/10-famous-parenting-quotes.

Chapter 5

1. Bly, David. Marcia Hill's *Yourparentingquestions.blogspot. com,* September 2, 2012, accessed December 9, 2013, http://www.more4kids.info/1020/Parenting-and-Motivational-Quotes-to-live-by.

Chapter 6

1. Plomp, John. Feb 15, 2007, *Smartbrief.com,* accessed December 8, 2013, http://www.smartbrief.com/02/15/07/you-know-children-are-growing-when-they-start-asking-questions-have-answers-1.UqYIxOIdB8A.

Chapter 7
1. Lair, Jess. *The Quotations Page,* compiled by compiled by M. Shawn Cole, accessed April 12, 2013, http://www. quotationspage.com/quote/26643.html.
2. Smalley, Gary. *Inspirational Quotes,* accessed December 8, 2013, http://www.inspirational-quotes-and-quotations.com/ quotes-about-parenting.html Quote Number Four.

Chapter 8
1. Adams, Samuel. *Brainyquote.com,* accessed April 12, 2013, http://www.brainyquote.com/quotes/authors/s/samuel_adams. html, Page 1.

Chapter 9
1. Virginia Satir. *Goodreads.com,* accessed on April 12, 2013, http://www.goodreads.com/quotes/151788.
2. Virginia Satir. *Brainyquote.com,* accessed December 8, 2013, www.brainyquote.com/quotes/authors/v/virginia satir.html.

Chapter 10
1. Holmes, Oliver Wendell. *Goodreads.com,* accessed December 8, 2013, http://www.goodreads.com/quotes/462803.
2. Faber, Adele and Elaine Mazlish. (2001). *Goodreads.com,* accessed April 12, 2013, http://www.goodreads.com/work/ quotes/2738870.

Chapter 11
1. Einstein, Albert. *Goodreads.com,* accessed April 12, 2013, http://www.goodreads.com/quotes/8241.

Chapter 12

1. Graham, Gordon. *Goodreads.com,* accessed April 12, 2013, www.goodreads.com/quotes/list/793094-lisa.

Chapter 13

1. Author Unknown. *PJ Media.com,* article by Dr. Helen Smith, accessed December 9, 2013, http://pjmedia.com/ drhelen/0/20139/0.

2. Author Unknown. *Net Industries,* accessed December 3, 2013, http://family.jrank.org/pages/1624/Spanking-Prevalence-Physical-Discipline.html" Spanking—Prevalence Of Physical Discipline/a.

Chapter 14

1. Alex Haley. *Brainyquote.com,* Alex Haley quotes, accessed April 12, 2013, www.brainyquote.com/quotes/authors/a/alex_haley.html.

Chapter 15

1. McTaggart, Jacquie. *Inspirational Words of Wisdom,* accessed December 3, 2013, http://www.wow4u.com/mctaggart2/index.html, Page 2.

Chapter 16

1. Van Buren, Abigail. *Pinterest.com, accessed December 3, 2013,* http://www.pinterest.com/kelleybrister/parenting-toward-independence/, Page 1.

BIBLIOGRAPHY

Baumrind, D. (1989). *Rearing competent children. In W. Damon (Ed.), Child Development Today and Tomorrow* (pp. 349-378). San Francisco: Jossey-Bass.

Dinkmeyer, Don Sr.,Gary D. McKay, an Don Dinkmeyes, Jr., (1997) *Systematic Training for Effective Parenting (STEP)* a series of books, Fredericksburg, VA: STEP Publishers.

Douglas, Ann. www.canadianparents.com/article/the-seven-deadly-sins.

Faber, Adele, and Elain Mazlish. *How To Talk To Kids So They Will Listen and How To Listen So Kids Will Talk.* Updated 2012, Scribner.

Keller, Phillip. *A Shepherd Looks at Psalm 23*, (1990),1970, pages 85-86 2 Keller, page 91

Ramirex, Laura. *Family Matters, Parenting Magazine, Stages of Child Development*, Copyright © 2009.

Wagner, Andres. *Hub Pages, Stages of Development—Teen Years, Tools for Stressless Living*, www.lifematters.com, June 6, 2008.

Edwards Brothers Malloy
Oxnard, CA USA
March 27, 2014